D1122784

CHRONICLES OF FAITH

JOSEPH

Rex Williams

Illustrated by
Al Bohl

BARBOUR
PUBLISHING

Cover illustration by Cory Godbey, Portland Studios, Inc.

Published by Barbour Publishing, Inc., P.O. Box 719, Uhrichsville, Ohio 44683, www.barbourbooks.com

Our mission is to publish and distribute inspirational products offering exceptional value and biblical encouragement to the masses.

 Member of the
Evangelical Christian
Publishers Association

Printed in the United States.

JOSEPH

Jacob dearly loved Joseph.

1

THE DREAMER

Now Joseph's father, Jacob, loved Joseph more than his other sons, because Joseph had been born when Jacob was an old man. When Joseph's brothers saw that Jacob loved Joseph more than them, they were no longer nice to their brother. They barely spoke to him at all, and when they did, it was usually only to be mean to him. To make matters worse, when Joseph saw his brothers ignoring their duties when they were supposed to be tending the sheep, he let his father know that the flocks were not being properly watched. While Jacob was glad to know Joseph wanted to see everything go well in the fields, Joseph's brothers only hated him all the more because of his meddling. Even though Jacob loved all his sons, the others were jealous of Joseph and treated him badly.

One day when Joseph was around seventeen years old, he had a strange dream. He told his brothers, "Listen to this dream I had: We were binding sheaves of grain out in the field when suddenly my sheaf rose and stood upright, while your sheaves gathered around mine and bowed down to it."

At this his brothers became even angrier with him. They said, "What! Do you intend to reign over us? Do you really think you will ever rule over us?" Joseph had gone too far this time. It was bad enough he had told their father when they had not been watching the sheep out in the field—what a dull, thankless job that was. But now, to have such a dream and then brag to them about it—that was even worse! "We'll take care of him first chance we get!"

Joseph's strange dream

But Joseph kept on dreaming his strange dreams. And, unfortunately, he kept telling his family about them, even though no one really wanted to hear about them any more. Not long after the first dream, he told his brothers, "Listen, I had another dream, and this time the sun and moon and eleven stars were bowing down to me." This seemed ridiculous to his brothers who by now were sick of hearing about Joseph's dreams.

But when he told his father, even Jacob got angry at the idea. "What is this dream you had? Will your mother and I and your brothers actually come and bow down to the ground before you?" Such dreams and ideas were very insulting in those days. Age was a sign of high honor—people didn't bow down to seventeen-year-old shepherd boys, especially not his father and older brothers!

Jacob is angry with Joseph.

With ten older brothers, Joseph and his younger brother, Benjamin, didn't have very much work to do. Their father was a rich man, and so they did not have to work to help make ends meet. They had many fun things to do. But often, the two youngest brothers were bored and looking for something to do. Joseph was glad when Jacob said to him one day, "As you know, your brothers are grazing the sheep near Shechem. I want you to go see them."

"All right, Father," Joseph replied.

So Jacob said, "Go and see if all is well with your brothers and with the flocks, and bring word back to me."

As Joseph prepared to leave, Benjamin begged, "Please, Joseph, take me with you."

But Joseph replied, "You know that Father doesn't like for both of us to be away from him at the same time. You are

Playing games

young yet; perhaps you may go next time." So Joseph left his home in the Hebron Valley and headed for Shechem.

But when Joseph got to Shechem, his brothers and the flocks were not there! After he had wandered the fields looking for them with no luck, a man saw him and asked him, "What are you looking for?"

Joseph answered, "I'm looking for my brothers. Can you tell me where they are grazing their flocks?"

The man knew Joseph's brothers and had spoken with them often. "They have moved on from here. I heard them say, 'Let's go to Dothan.'"

Joseph thanked the man and set out for Dothan. But his older brothers saw him and recognized him while he was still a long way off.

"Here comes that dreamer!" they sneered

"Here comes that dreamer."

to each other. "Come on, let's kill him and throw him into one of these cisterns and say that a ferocious animal devoured him. *Then* we'll see what comes of his dreams!"

Most of the brothers were in total agreement—they were sick to death of Joseph being Jacob's favorite and getting all the attention with his strange dreams. Jealousy burned hot within their hearts. They were sure that no one would ever find a dead body in one of the dozens of cisterns out in the open wilderness where they were grazing their flocks. They would be able to kill Joseph without anyone ever finding out they had done it.

But Reuben, the oldest, had pity in his heart for Joseph and tried to save the boy from his jealous brothers' schemes. He knew he could not win a fight against all the others, so he decided to act as if he were in agreement with them.

"Let's say an animal killed him."

"Let's not take his life," he said. "Our Law forbids the shedding of blood. Just throw him into this cistern here in the wilderness, and don't lay a hand on him. This way he'll die, but we won't shed his blood."

Reuben planned to sneak away from the camp in the middle of the night, pull his brother out, and send him back home to Jacob. He was sure that Joseph would keep silent about the whole thing since Reuben had saved his life—and maybe Joseph might keep his dreams to himself from then on.

Now Joseph was wearing a beautifully decorated robe his father had made especially for him. It was a very special robe and had caused much jealousy among his brothers when it was given to Joseph. When he came up to where his brothers were standing, four

Attacking Joseph

of them grabbed him and held him down while the others stripped the robe from him.

Joseph cried out, "What are you doing, my brothers?"

They answered, "We've heard enough of your stupid dreams! Let's see what kind of dreams you dream in the bottom of this cistern!"

When Joseph saw that his brothers were not simply playing a trick on him but meant to leave him to die in the cistern, he cried out for help. But there was no one to hear him in that remote place. They threw him into a cistern that had no water in it, only the limestone walls and bottom.

By this time it was evening, and the brothers sat down to their meal. Reuben, as the oldest, took charge of posting the guards over the sheep for the night and

Putting Joseph in the cistern

seeing that all was in order in the camp. While he was doing this, the other brothers saw a caravan of Midianites approaching on their way to Egypt. They were carrying precious spices to trade in Egypt for gold and silver.

Judah said to the other brothers, "You know, Joseph is our brother after all, our own flesh and blood; what good would it be to us if we kill him? Instead, let's sell him to the Midianites as a slave. That way we can get rid of him without ever being guilty of murdering our own brother." The other brothers thought about this and agreed it was better.

As the caravan of Midianite merchants drew near, Judah called out to them, "Hello, travelers! What news from the north?"

The Midianites spoke pleasantly to Joseph's brothers in return, and soon they

"We can always sell a slave."

had a friendly conversation going. Judah then casually mentioned, "Oh, by the way, you wouldn't be interested in purchasing a slave for the Egyptian market, would you?"

The Midianite in charge of the caravan replied, "Why, yes, we can always sell a slave for a good profit in Egypt."

The brothers promptly hauled Joseph up out of the cistern and handed him over, bound and gagged, to the Midianites for twenty silver coins. But Joseph's brothers kept the beautiful robe that their father Jacob had given him. They had a plan in mind for it.

When Reuben returned from making the rounds of the camp, he went to look in on Joseph in the cistern. In the fading light he could not be sure, but he didn't think he saw Joseph. He decided to wait

Handing Joseph over to slavery

until later in the night to pull Joseph out and send him home.

Later, however, he crept to the cistern in the early hours of the morning to set Joseph free. He called, softly at first and then much louder, "Joseph—Joseph, it is I, Reuben. I will pull you out and set you free!" But when he heard no answer, he went and asked his brothers, "Where is the boy Joseph?"

They replied, "While you were out, we sold him to a Midianite caravan bound for Egypt. He will not trouble us anymore!" When Reuben heard this, he tore his clothes in grief for the boy and for his father, whom he knew loved Joseph greatly.

Tearing his clothes

"Is this Joseph's?"

2

THE SLAVE

The brothers agreed that they could not tell their father the truth about what they had done—even Reuben agreed that their wicked act had to be covered up. So they took Joseph's robe and dipped it in the blood of a goat they had killed. When they returned home several days later, they went sadly to their father and asked, "Has Joseph been sent out from the house while we were tending the flocks in the wilderness?"

Jacob, who had been growing more worried with each passing day, said anxiously, "Why, yes, I sent him out to see how it went with you. Didn't you see him?"

"No," they lied, "but we found this two days ago. Look and see whether it is your son Joseph's."

When Jacob saw that it was indeed the very robe he had given Joseph, he said, "It is my son's robe! Some ferocious animal has devoured him. Joseph has surely been torn to pieces."

Jacob went into mourning for his lost son Joseph. As was the custom of his people, he tore his clothes, put on sackcloth, and mourned for many days. All his sons and his daughters came to comfort him, but his sense of loss over his favorite son was very great. He could not be comforted. In the depths of his sorrow, he wept for many days over his son.

When Jacob's family tried to comfort him, he replied, "No, in mourning will I go down to the grave to my son." And his other sons began to deeply regret the evil they had done.

Meanwhile, Joseph, very much alive, was being carried farther and farther away from

"It is my son's robe."

the home he had always known. He was a brave lad, but at seventeen he was little more than a boy and was very frightened. He had heard about the slave trade in Egypt. Many slaves died or were treated poorly by their masters. Most worked too long in the hot sun for a few short years until their strength left them and their health failed, and then they were abandoned or put to death. He was almost overcome with fear as he thought of dying in a strange land, never seeing his father or Benjamin again. But in the depths of fear and despair Joseph's faith in the God of his father began to deepen.

Joseph remembered the stories his father had told of how he, Jacob, had personally wrestled with God all night long on a riverbank until God had given him a blessing. Jacob had told him of the promises the Lord had made to Jacob's father, Isaac, as well as to Jacob himself.

Slave caravan

Joseph remembered how Jacob had always assured him that God would never fail him nor leave him to face trouble alone. And Joseph began to pray.

"Lord," he said, "I don't know what will happen to me. I'm alone, I'm scared, and I don't know what tomorrow will bring. I miss my father and my home and my warm bed. I don't understand why You have let this happen, Lord; but I trust You to protect me. I place my life in Your hands." Somewhat reassured, Joseph finally managed to drop off to sleep.

The journey to Egypt took several weeks through rugged wilderness and desert. The Midianites laughed when Joseph told them it was his brothers who had sold him into slavery.

"If that's so, boy, it doesn't change anything. You'll fetch a good price in the market. We must get our investment back on you!"

Joseph was sold to an Egyptian named

"Lord, I trust You to protect me."

Potiphar, who was the captain of the guard for Pharaoh, the king of Egypt. The Lord was with Joseph in everything he did, and as a result, Potiphar prospered as well. Potiphar, a shrewd man, saw that the Lord's hand was on Joseph for good. So he said, "Joseph, I will set you over all my affairs. I know your God will bless all that you do." So the Lord blessed all of Potiphar's affairs because of Joseph.

The years passed and Joseph grew to be a handsome young man. Potiphar's wife began to notice him. She flirted with Joseph and tried to get him to neglect his work in order to spend more time with her. But Joseph said, "How can I flirt with you and spend time with you when I should be working? It would be very ungrateful toward your husband for me to do such a thing."

At this rejection, Potiphar's wife became angry and cried out, "Help! Help! This Hebrew

Potiphar buying Joseph

slave has sneaked into the house to do me harm! Help! Help!" She was lying in order to get even with Joseph for rejecting her.

When Potiphar heard the story from his wife, he said to Joseph, "So this is how you repay me for setting you over all my affairs! I will do to you as you have done to me." Turning to his guardsmen, he said, "Throw him in prison!"

Potiphar had chosen to believe his wife instead of a Hebrew slave like Joseph. So Joseph found himself once again mistreated at the hands of others.

In the prison, Joseph prayed every day to the Lord. "My God, I don't understand how this could have happened. I was a source of blessing, by Your grace, for all Potiphar's family. And it was for *refusing* to do wrong toward Potiphar that I have ended up in prison. I don't understand why You have let

"Help! Help!"

this happen to me. Should I have done evil so I could have stayed out of prison?"

But the Lord encouraged Joseph and blessed him even in prison. The Lord gave him favor with the warden so that he set Joseph over all the affairs of the prison, just as Potiphar had done in his house. All that Joseph did in prison went well.

In prison

The years in prison dragged by.

3

STRANGE VISIONS

The laws of Egypt did not bother too much about protecting slaves, and it looked to Joseph as if he would spend the rest of his life in prison. The days dragged into weeks, the weeks into months, and the months into years. And yet Joseph, a man like you and me, did one simple thing: He put his trust in God. He remembered the stories his father, Jacob, told about seeing God face to face; he remembered how God had made promises to Abraham, Isaac, and Jacob; he remembered the mighty things those men had seen God do for them in the face of trouble; and although he often worried, he never gave up hope. He trusted that the Lord over all the earth would do the right thing, and he prayed often to God. And then one day something strange happened.

It seems that both the king's cupbearer and his baker had somehow offended Egypt's king, who was called Pharaoh. He was quite angry with each of them and said to the captain of the guard, "Throw them in the guardhouse!"

The cupbearer was head over all the people who served food and drink in the king's household, and the baker was the chief baker for Pharaoh. They had failed at their duties and greatly angered Pharaoh, and he had them thrown into prison while he decided what he would do to them. In those days, kings did pretty much as they wished—there was no system of laws like many modern countries have. So the chief baker and the chief cupbearer were very afraid as they were put into prison. The captain of the guard put them under Joseph's care.

"Throw them in the prison!"

After they had been in the prison for some time, the chief cupbearer had a certain dream, and it greatly troubled him as he tried to figure out what it might mean. On the same night, the chief baker had a dream, and he, too, was quite worried over what his dream might mean.

As the two men were pondering their dreams and wondering whether they had any special meaning, Joseph came in to bring them breakfast. When he saw the two men he asked them, "Why are your faces so sad today?"

They replied, "We both had dreams, but there is no one to interpret them."

"Do not interpretations belong to God?" Joseph said. "Tell me your dreams and, by the grace of God, perhaps I will be able to give you the interpretation of them."

"Why are you so sad?"

"I will go first," said Pharaoh's chief cup-bearer. "In my dream I saw a vine in front of me, and on the vine were three branches. As soon as it budded, it blossomed, and its clusters ripened into grapes. Pharaoh's cup was in my hand, and I took the grapes, squeezed them into Pharaoh's cup and put the cup into his hand."

"What do you think it can mean?" asked the baker, now even more worried about his own dream.

"The Lord will give me the proper meaning, if He so wills," replied Joseph. "I will tell you as soon as I know what the interpretation is. Perhaps these dreams have meant nothing in particular. But we will certainly see."

Later that day, Joseph returned to the two men. "Well," the cupbearer asked anxiously, "what does it mean?"

"This is what it means," Joseph replied.

"Three branches means three days."

"The three branches are three days. Within three days Pharaoh will lift you up and restore you to your former position, and you will put Pharaoh's cup in his hand, just as you used to do when you were his cupbearer. But when all goes well with you, remember me and show me kindness; mention me to Pharaoh and get me out of this prison. For I was forcibly carried off from the land of the Hebrews, and even here I have done nothing to deserve being put in a prison."

The two men were amazed that Joseph had been able to interpret the dream, and the chief cupbearer thanked him many times.

When the chief baker saw that the cupbearer's dream had been a good sign, he took heart and asked Joseph about his dream. "I, too, had a dream: On my head were three baskets of bread. In the top basket were all kinds of baked goods for Pharaoh, but the

"I, too, had a dream."

birds were eating them out of the basket on my head."

After praying about the dream, Joseph went back to the baker and said, "This is what your dream means: The three baskets are three days. Within three days Pharaoh will take off your head and hang you on a tree. And the birds will eat away your flesh."

When he heard this, the chief baker was terrified. He begged Joseph to give another interpretation, but Joseph said, "I am sorry, but I can only say what the Lord has given me to say."

Three days later was Pharaoh's birthday, and he decided to throw a huge party for all his servants and the members of his court. At a great ceremony in the presence of all his most important officials, Pharaoh did indeed bring his chief cupbearer and his chief baker out of prison. Pharaoh restored the chief cup

Terrified!

bearer to his former position, so that he again put the cup into the hands of Pharaoh, just as Joseph had prophesied. But the chief baker he hanged, just as the dream had foretold.

So Joseph's interpretations of both dreams came true. And although the chief cup-bearer had been very grateful to Joseph when he heard the favorable interpretation of his dream, in the excitement of being restored to his former position, he forgot his promise to mention Joseph to Pharaoh.

So Joseph stayed in prison. The days, weeks and months seemed to drag on forever, and Joseph often cried out, "O mighty God, why have you let this happen to me? Have you forgotten me completely?"

Two more years passed. Then one night, Pharaoh had a dream. In the dream, Pharaoh was standing by the Nile River, when seven fat, healthy cows came out of the river and began

Pharaoh's dream

grazing on the reeds at the river's edge. After these seven came seven other cows that were thin, scrawny, and ugly. The thin, ugly cows stood beside the fat, healthy cows on the river-bank. Then the seven thin, ugly cows ate up the sleek, fat cows.

Then Pharaoh awoke from his dream in the middle of the night, and sat up in his bed. "What a strange dream!" he said to himself.

But shortly after that Pharaoh fell asleep again, and again he began to dream. This time in his dream seven full, healthy heads of grain were growing on one stalk. After these seven, seven other heads of grain sprouted—wasted, parched, and withered by the east wind. Then, just as in the other dream, the seven parched and withered heads of grain swallowed up the seven healthy, full heads of grain.

Once again Pharaoh awoke and sat up

"What a strange dream!"

in his bed. "What a strange night this has been!" he exclaimed. "I have had not one, but two dreams that are alike and yet not alike. Surely these dreams must mean something." Pharaoh did not believe in the God of Joseph's forefathers—Pharaoh thought there were many different kinds of gods and that one of these had sent him the dreams.

"Surely these dreams must mean something."

The cupbearer and the pharaoh

4

FAMINE!

In the morning, Pharaoh said to his wise men and magicians, "I have had two strange dreams. Interpret them for me, because I am troubled by them." But when he had told them the dreams, none could interpret them.

Then the chief cupbearer said to Pharaoh, "Today I am reminded of my shortcomings. Pharaoh was once angry with his servants, and he imprisoned me and the chief baker in the house of the captain of the guard. Each of us had a dream the same night, and each dream had a meaning of its own. Now a young Hebrew was there with us, a servant of the captain of the guard. We told him our dreams, and he interpreted them for us, giving each man the interpretation of his dream. And things turned out exactly as he interpreted them to us: I was restored to my position, and the other man was hanged."

When he heard this, Pharaoh commanded the captain of the guard, "Bring this man Joseph out of the dungeon." When Joseph had bathed and changed his clothes, they brought him before Pharaoh.

Pharaoh said to Joseph, "I had a dream, and no one can interpret is. But I have heard it said of you that when you hear a dream you can interpret it."

"I cannot do it," Joseph replied, "but God will give Pharaoh the answer he desires."

Then Pharaoh explained the two dreams to Joseph and said, "I told this to my magicians and wise men, but none of them could explain the meaning to me. Can your God give you the interpretation of these things?"

"Yes, O King," said Joseph, "the dreams of Pharaoh are one and the same. God has

Joseph before the pharaoh

revealed to Pharaoh what He is about to do. The seven good cows are seven years, and the seven good heads of grain are seven years. The seven lean, ugly cows are seven years, and so are the seven worthless heads of grain scorched by the east wind: They are seven years of famine.

"God has shown Pharaoh that seven years of great plenty are coming through the land of Egypt, but seven years of famine will follow them. Then all the abundance in Egypt will be forgotten, because the famine that follows will be so severe. The reason the dream was given to Pharaoh in two forms is that the matter has been firmly decided, and God will do it soon."

Then Joseph said, "And now let Pharaoh look for a wise man and put him in charge of the land of Egypt. Let Pharaoh appoint commissioners over the land to take a fifth

"God will do it soon!"

of all Egypt's harvest during the seven good years. They should collect all the food of these good years that are coming and store the grain under the authority of Pharaoh, to be kept in the cities for food. This food should be held in reserve for the country, to be used during the seven years of famine, so the country will not be ruined by the famine."

Pharaoh and his men agreed with Joseph's plan. Then Pharaoh said to his advisers, "Can we find anyone like this man, one in whom is the Spirit of God?" And they agreed that no one could be found like Joseph.

So right then and there, Pharaoh said to Joseph, "Since God has made all this known to you, there is no one as wise as you. You will be in charge of my palace, and all my people must obey your orders. Only the fact that I am the king will give me more power than I am now giving to you."

"Can we find anyone like this man?"

Pharaoh then took off his special ring and said to Joseph, "I hereby put you in charge of the whole land of Egypt." He put the ring on Joseph's finger, dressed him in fine linen robes, and put a gold chain around his neck. Pharaoh had Joseph ride in a chariot as his second-in-command, and the people shouted, "Make way!" when he rode through.

Pharaoh said to Joseph, "I am still pharaoh, but in everything else, no one will lift a hand or foot in all Egypt without your approval." Pharaoh renamed him Zaphenath-Paneah and gave him the beautiful Asenath to be his wife.

Now Joseph was thirty years old when all these things happened, and he went out and began to travel around Egypt as the second-in-command to Pharaoh.

During the seven good years that God

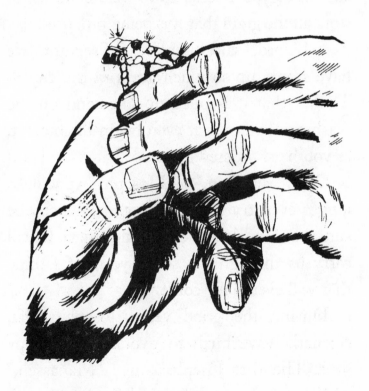

"You are in charge of the land of Egypt."

had foretold in Pharaoh's dream, the land produced huge amounts of every crop. Joseph supervised a massive storage effort for the entire land of Egypt. Special cities were built just to store all the grain that was being produced.

"My lord," said Joseph's chief servant, "we have stored up so much grain in the city of Thebes that it is piled up like sand on the seashore—we cannot even begin to count it, as you have ordered us to do."

"Very well then," said Joseph, "we will no longer even try to keep a count. We can be sure that God is blessing us and that He will carry us through the seven years of famine that will eventually come."

During the good years, Joseph's wife, Asenath, gave birth to two healthy, happy sons. The first Joseph named "Manasseh," which sounds means "forget." For Joseph said,

Storing the grain

"Now God has made me forget all my trouble and all my father's household." The second son Joseph named "Ephraim," which means "twice fruitful." He said, "It is because God has made me fruitful in the land where I once suffered."

But after seven years of plenty, the famine hit Egypt and all the nearby countries, just as God foretold through Joseph. The nearby countries began to feel the famine, because they had not been warned as Egypt had. But in Egypt there was food. As the famine got worse, the Egyptian people came to Pharaoh for help, and he said, "Do as Joseph tells you."

Soon the famine had spread throughout the entire country of Egypt, and it became time for Joseph to use the wisdom and guidance that the Lord had given him for just such troubled times. Joseph had all the great storehouses in each city opened up, and the

Seven years of famine

grain that had been brought in from the surrounding fields and stored in each city was ready to be sold to all the people. Pharaoh had taken one-fifth of all the crops produced in the land during the good years as a tax on the farmers. Now Pharaoh had grain and other produce to sell to the Egyptian people to keep them alive. Not only that, but all the neighboring countries came to Egypt to buy grain and other supplies, because the famine was very bad all over that part of the world. Only Egypt had been prepared, thanks to Joseph's God.

Jacob, Joseph's father, soon learned back in Canaan that Egypt still had grain that it was willing to sell to other people. He said to his remaining sons, "Why are you sitting around looking at each other? I hear that there is grain for sale in Egypt. Go down there and buy some for us so that we will not die."

Buying grain from Egypt

Jacob sent the ten older brothers to Egypt to buy grain. But he did not send Benjamin, the youngest, because Benjamin had become his favorite after Joseph had disappeared, and he was afraid that something bad might happen to Benjamin also. So Jacob's sons went down to Egypt, along with other people of every description, because only Egypt still had grain to sell.

It so happened that Joseph, as the governor of the land under Pharaoh, was the one in charge of selling grain both to the Egyptians and to those from other countries. Imagine his surprise when one day, ten dusty, bearded Hebrews stumbled in, tired from their long journey, and bowed down to him with their faces to the ground!

"O great Zaphenath-Paneah, governor of all Egypt," they said, "please allow your humble servants to buy some grain for our starving families." They did not recognize

Jacob's sons going to Egypt

him, because it had been many years since they last saw him, and he had grown to manhood—but Joseph recognized his brothers.

"Where do you come from?" he asked through an interpreter, speaking sternly and pretending to be a stranger.

They replied, "We have come from the land of Canaan to buy food." It was then that Joseph remembered his dreams about his brothers bowing down to him. The dreams had come to pass, but he felt no joy about it. He decided to test his brothers to see what kind of men they had become.

"You are spies!" he cried. "You have come to see where our land is unprotected!"

"No, my lord, we only want food. We are honest men, all sons of one man. Our youngest brother is with our father in Canaan, and one brother is no more."

"Well then, here is how I will test you.

"You are spies!"

You must go back and bring this young-est brother to me. One of you will be kept in prison till the rest of you return. If you are lying, I will know you are spies!" But he threw them all in prison first.

"Bring your youngest brother here!"

"Surely we are being punished."

5

JOSEPH'S TEST

Joseph let his brothers stew in prison for three days. On the third day, he had them brought before him and spoke to them again.

"Do this and you will live," he told them, "for I fear God and will act fairly. If you are honest men, let one of your brothers stay here in prison while the rest of you go and take grain back for your starving households. But you must bring your youngest brother to me so that your words may be proved true and that you may not die."

Then Joseph's brothers began to talk among themselves, believing that as an Egyptian he could not understand their speech because he had been speaking to them through an interpreter. They said, "Surely we are being punished by the Lord because of what we did to Joseph."

"We saw how distressed Joseph was when he pleaded with us for his life, but we wouldn't listen. That's why this distress has come upon us."

"Didn't I tell you not to sin against the boy?" asked Reuben. "But you wouldn't listen. Now we must give an accounting for the blood we spilled."

Joseph had to turn has back to his brothers, he was so overcome with emotion at hearing that they had repented and were sorry that they had done such an evil thing to him so many years before. He wept silently with a mixture of grief and joy—grief that he had ever had to be taken away from his family by the cruel thing his brothers had done, and joy that they had become men of character who were able to learn from their mistakes and to repent of them before the Lord.

Weeping for joy and grief

But then Joseph stopped weeping, dried his eyes, and turned to face his brothers once again. He was not through testing them—not yet. He had his brother Simeon taken from them by his guards, and right in front of them had him placed in chains.

"In this way will your words be tested to see if you are telling the truth," he said to them. "If you are not, then as surely as Pharaoh lives, you are spies! I will keep this one while you return to Canaan and feed your starving families. But then you must return to Egypt, and you had better bring this youngest brother back with you."

His brothers again began to protest their innocence, saying, "My lord, it is just as we have told you—"

But Joseph cut them off and would not hear any more.

"Go now and prepare to return to Canaan.

Chaining Simeon

Your brother will be kept safely here until you return. You need not fear for him, if you are telling the truth. But if you are lying then you will not see my face in order to speak with me again."

Joseph spoke to the men who attended him, "Fill each man's bags with grain, as much as they will hold, and give each man all the provisions he will need for the journey back to Canaan." And then, calling the chief steward aside, he spoke quietly. "I want you to place each man's silver, that they have given in payment, back in his sack of grain."

All these commands were carried out by Joseph's men. As soon as all the preparations were completed, Joseph's brothers left for Canaan.

After a long day's journey, Joseph's nine remaining brothers stopped to rest for the night. As one of the brothers opened one of

Joseph and the chief steward

the sacks to get some grain out to feed his donkey, he saw a small bag in the mouth of the sack.

"What could this be?" he wondered out loud, and pulled the sack from the larger sack of grain. He opened the drawstring, and out into his open hand tumbled several silver coins from the land of Canaan!

Astonished, he ran back to the campfire with the silver and said in a quavering voice, "My silver has been returned. Here it is in my sack!"

The men did not know what to make of this and turned to each other in great confusion and fear. Their hearts sank as they wondered, "What is this that God has done to us?" Yet no one thought then to search their bags further.

When the nine brothers returned to their father Jacob, they told him all about their trip

Silver coins

and the strange things that had happened. They said, "The man who is lord over the land spoke harshly to us and treated us as though we were spying on their land. We denied it and explained to him that we are all brothers, and that we are honest men.

"Then the man who is lord over the land said to us, 'This is how I will know whether you are honest men: Leave one of your brothers here with me, and take food for your starving households and go. But bring your youngest brother to me so I will know that you are not spies but honest men. Then I will give your brother back to you, and you can trade in the land.'"

Then, as they began to unpack from the journey, each man found in his sack his pouch of silver that had been given in payment for the grain in Egypt! They all became frightened, and Jacob said, "You

Explaining their problem to Jacob

have deprived me of my children. Joseph is no more and Simeon is no more, and now you want to take Benjamin. Everything is against me!"

Then Reuben, the eldest, replied, "You may put both of my sons to death if I do not bring Benjamin back to you. Entrust him to my care, and I will bring him back."

But Jacob said, "My son will not go down to Egypt with you. Now that Joseph is dead, Benjamin is the only one I have left. If harm comes to him on the journey you are taking, it will bring my gray head down to the grave in sorrow."

The family of Jacob could not agree on what to do next, so they did nothing. But the famine continued throughout the land so that finally Jacob instructed his sons, "Go back and see if you can't buy just a little more grain in Egypt."

"Entrust Benjamin to my care."

But Judah said to him, "The man there warned us sternly, 'You will not see me to talk to me again unless your brother is with you.' If you send Benjamin along with us, we will go down and buy food for all the families. But if you won't let Benjamin come with us, there is no point in going, because the man will not speak to us unless we bring our youngest brother."

At this the old man Jacob wrung his hands and cried out in sorrow. "Why must my sons be taken from me?"

Jacob wept aloud in distress over the problem he had to face. Then he turned to his sons and shouted, "Why did you bring this trouble on me by telling the man you had another brother?"

"It is not really our fault, Father," replied Asher soothingly. "This Egyptian questioned us in great detail about ourselves and

"Why must my sons be taken from me?"

our family. He asked, 'Is your father still living? Do you have another brother?' All we did was answer his questions; we could hardly have done otherwise. He would not have sold us the grain if we had been unwilling to answer his questions. We simply answered the questions he put to us. How were we to know he would say to us, 'Bring your brother down here'?" And all Asher's brothers said the same thing to their father.

Then Judah spoke up. He said, "Send the boy Benjamin along with me and we will go at once, so that we and you and our many children may continue to live and not die in this famine. I will guarantee his safety; you can hold me personally responsible for him. If I do not bring him back to you safe and sound and set him down right here in front of you, I will bear the blame before you all the rest of my life. But as it is right now with all this talk, we

"I will guarantee his safety."

could have been there and back again twice by now if we hadn't delayed."

All the brothers began to talk at once so that no one could make himself understood above the others. Finally Jacob raised his hand to silence them. "I have made my decision," he announced.

"You, Reuben, and you, Judah, know more than anyone else what Joseph and now Benjamin have meant to me. And you two have been willing to put up your own sons and your honor for Benjamin so that you may buy back Simeon and bring back grain so that we will not starve. It pleases me to know that you have begun to follow the God of your forefathers and to do what is good and right, no matter what the cost. I will tell you now that I have often wondered whether you would be God-fearing men or not, and I have not always

"I have made my decision."

believed everything you told me."

The brothers hung their heads in shame at this, since they knew he was speaking about what they had told him about Joseph.

Then Jacob paused and drew a long breath. "So, if it must be, I will entrust Benjamin to you two, though I fear I will yet lose him. Take the best products of our land down to the man as a gift—a little honey, balm, some spices and myrrh, pistachio nuts, and almonds. And take double the silver back with you, since you will have to return the silver we found in the mouths of your sacks. Perhaps it was a mistake. Take your brother Benjamin also and go back to the man at once. And may God Almighty grant you mercy before the man so that he will let Simeon and Benjamin come back with you." Then the old man began to weep again under

"I have not always believed you."

the great pain of seeing his youngest being carried away to face this powerful stranger. "But as for me," he said, "I am bereaved, I am bereaved."

"I am bereaved."

"He wants to attack us."

6

More Trouble

Although the brothers tried to console their father, they could not. So they took the gifts, all the silver, and their youngest brother Benjamin, and hurried back down to Egypt to present themselves before Joseph.

When Joseph saw that Benjamin was with them, he told his steward, "Take these men to my house and prepare the noon meal for me to eat with them."

But Joseph's brothers did not understand the command he gave, since he spoke in Egyptian. So when they came to his house, they thought to themselves, "He is bringing us here because of the silver that was put into our sacks the first time. He wants to attack us and overpower us, take our donkeys, and make us his slaves so that he can recover the money he lost when we somehow had the silver put back into our bags!"

So immediately the brothers spoke up to the steward, saying, "Please, sir; we came down here the first time to buy food. But at the first place we camped for the night, we opened our sacks and each of us found our silver, the exact amount, in the mouth of his sack. So we have brought it back with us. We have also brought additional silver with us to buy more food. We don't know who put our silver in our sacks."

The steward, who had returned their silver at Joseph's orders, knew Joseph did not mean to harm them. He reassured them. "It's all right," he said, "don't be afraid. Your God, the God of your father, has given you treasure in your sacks; I myself received the silver you gave last time. And now," he continued, "I have a surprise for you."

"God has given you a treasure."

The steward snapped his fingers at a servant waiting nearby, who disappeared into the interior of the house. In a few moments he returned, leading Simeon into the front room!

"My brothers, my beloved brothers!" he beamed. "I knew you would return for me."

"How have you been? How were you treated?" they all asked at once, still nervous about how they would be received by this stern Egyptian and wondering about the silver in their sacks.

"Oh, fine, fine!" he said cheerfully. "Zaphenath-Paneah is a busy man, yet he has come to speak with me through an interpreter once a week since you left. He asks me everything about our families, our wives, and children. I have really been under house arrest here—I've not been in the prison."

The brothers were surprised to hear

"My beloved brothers!"

that Simeon had not been kept in the prison, and they were frightened to hear that the stern Egyptian governor had been finding out even more about their families. What would he demand of them next?

The steward then took the brothers into Joseph's house and gave them water to wash their feet and gave them food for their donkeys. He told them they would be eating with Joseph at noon, so they made their gifts ready to present to him when he arrived.

When Joseph came home, they presented to him the gifts they had brought, and again his brothers all bowed low before him, their faces touching the ground. He began by asking them how they were.

"We have been fine, my lord, except that the famine continues," they replied.

"How is your aged father you told me about? Is he still living?" They did not notice

Bowing before Joseph

how the man anxiously leaned forward as he asked this question.

"Your servant our father is still alive and well." And again they bowed before him to show him honor.

As his eyes lit upon Benjamin, his beloved brother, he asked, "Is this your youngest brother, the one you told me about?" And he said, "God be gracious to you, my son." Joseph became greatly moved as he looked upon the face of his most beloved younger brother, whom he had not seen for so long. He had to quickly excuse himself from their presence and hurry outside to find a place to weep in secret.

After Joseph had managed to bring himself under control, he washed his face and returned to the dining hall. "Serve the food," he said.

According to the practices of the Egyptians,

Quickly excusing himself

Joseph was served by himself, the Egyptians at the meal were served by themselves, and Joseph's brothers were served at yet another table, because Egyptians did not like to eat at the same table as Hebrews. His brothers were astonished to see that they had been seated at the table in the order of their ages. "How did he know who was the oldest and who came next in order?" They asked one another. And when they were finally served their food, Benjamin received five times as much as any-one else at their table. All Joseph's brothers had a good time at the feast and laughed and talked freely.

"My honored guests, men of Canaan," Joseph began, when the time for speeches came, "I have tested you to see whether indeed you were honest men, as you claimed"—here he paused dramatically for effect—"and I am pleased to see that you have in no way

Benjamin receiving the most food

disappointed me." All of Joseph's brothers breathed a sigh of relief.

"You are indeed honest men, sons of one father, and not spies, as I had originally feared. Please accept my apologies and be assured that, in the morning, you will all be free to depart and return with all haste to your families in Canaan, who I am sure are waiting for the food that you will bring them."

Reuben, the oldest, arose after Joseph's speech had been fully translated and said, "Thank you, my lord. We will do as you say."

But as his brothers were packing the next morning, Joseph said to his steward, "Fill each sack completely, and again put each man's silver in the mouth of his sack. Then put my special silver cup in the mouth of the youngest one's sack." And the steward did as he was told.

Shortly after his brothers set out, Joseph

"We will do as you say."

sent the steward after them, saying, "When you catch up to them, say, 'Why have you repaid good with evil? Isn't this the cup my master drinks from and also uses for divination? This is a wicked thing you have done.'"

So the steward and his men rode furiously after Joseph's brothers and soon caught up with them and stopped them. And when they halted the caravan, the steward confronted Reuben and repeated the words Joseph had given him to say.

But when they were confronted by the steward in this manner, Joseph's brothers became very angry.

"Why does my lord say such things? Far be it from your servants to do anything like that! We even brought back to you from the land of Canaan the silver we found inside the mouths of our sacks! So why would we steal silver or gold from your master's house?

Joseph's stewards stopping the caravan

If any of your servants is found to have it, he will die; and the rest of us will become your slaves."

Now this was a foolish thing for Joseph's brothers to say, even if they were angry and very sure that none of them had done such a thing. They had quickly forgotten the strange events of their first trip and the silver in their sacks!

"Rash words indeed," said the steward, "but I will hold you to them! Let it be as you say. Whoever is found to have the cup will become my slave; the rest of you will be free from blame."

Each of the brothers quickly took his sack down from his donkey and opened it for inspection. Then the steward searched each sack in turn, beginning with Reuben and ending with Benjamin, the youngest. And, of course, the cup was found in Benjamin's sack, right where the steward had put it!

"Why would we steal?"

The brothers, astonished, tore their clothes in grief. Silently, they each mounted their donkeys and returned to the city, determined to keep their youngest brother from becoming the slave of a foreign master.

The cup

At Joseph's mercy

7

Reunion!

Joseph's brothers came before him in his house and threw themselves at his feet. He said to them, "What is this you have done? Don't you know a man like me can find things out by divination?" He said this to frighten them. Joseph did not really practice divination, since it was an evil thing. Joseph got all his guidance from the Lord.

"What can we say to my lord?" said Judah. "How can we prove our innocence? God has uncovered your servants' guilt. We are now my lord's slaves—we ourselves and the one who was found to have the cup." Judah would rather have become a slave in a foreign country than have to go back and face his father after losing Benjamin.

But Joseph said, "Only the thief will be my slave; the rest may go."

Then Judah came closer and asked, "Please let me have a word with you. You asked us, my lord, about our family, and we told you about our aged father and our youngest brother, much loved by our father. Then you said to your servants, 'Bring him down to me so I can see him for myself.' And we said to you, 'The boy cannot leave his father; if he leaves him, his father will die.' But you told us, your servants, 'Unless your youngest brother comes down with you, you will not see my face again.' When we went back to our father, we told him what you had said.

"When our father sent us back to get more grain this time, we warned him, 'We cannot go down. Only if Benjamin is with us will we go. We cannot see the man's face unless our youngest brother is with us.'

"So now, if the boy is not with us when I

Telling Joseph their story

go back to my father and if my father, whose life is closely bound up with the boy's life, sees that the boy isn't there, he will die. We will have brought the gray head of our father down to the grave in sorrow. I, your servant, guaranteed the boy's safety to my father. I said, 'If I do not bring him back to you, I will bear the blame before you all my life!'

"Now then, please let your servant remain here as my lord's slave in place of the boy, and let the boy return with his brothers. How can I go back to my father if the boy is not with me? No! Do not let me see the misery that would come upon my father." So Judah offered to take his brother's place as a slave in a strange country, to spare his father grief.

When Joseph saw the great sacrifice that Judah, who had formerly treated him so badly, was willing to make for his father and

"I will bear the blame."

for Benjamin, he could stand it no longer. "Have everyone leave my presence!" he cried. Joseph wept so loudly that the Egyptians heard him even outside the room, and they told Pharaoh's household about it later.

Joseph then cried out to his brothers, in their own Hebrew language, "I am Joseph!" They stared at him, stricken with shock and amazement.

"Is my father still living?" he asked, hardly daring to hope that it could be so, since Jacob had been an old man when Joseph had been carried off so many years before. But his brothers were so terrified of him that they couldn't answer.

Then Joseph said to them, "Come close to me," and they did so. Then he said, "I am indeed your brother Joseph, the one you sold into Egypt! And now, do not be distressed and do not be angry with yourselves

"I am Joseph!"

for selling me here, because it was to save lives that God sent me ahead of you. For two years now there has been a famine in the land, and for the next five years there will not be any farming. But God sent me ahead of you to preserve for you a remnant on earth and to save your lives by a great deliverance.

"So then, it was not you who sent me here, but God. He made me a representative of Pharaoh, lord of his entire household, and ruler of all Egypt. Now hurry back to my father and give him this message."

Then Joseph told them, "Say to Jacob, 'This is what your son Joseph said, "God has made me lord of all Egypt. Come down to me; don't delay. You shall live in the region of Goshen and be near me—you, your children and grandchildren, your flocks and herds, and all you have. I will provide

"It was to save lives that God sent me here."

for you there, because five years of famine are still to come. Otherwise you and your household and all who belong to you will become poor.'"

"You can see for yourselves, and so can my brother Benjamin, that it is really I who am speaking to you. Tell my father about all the honor accorded me in Egypt and about everything you have seen. And bring my father down here quickly."

For a long moment they all continued to stare at Joseph in silence.

Then, all at once, the joy of being reunited with his family—and of being restored to them as a true brother and not an enemy—completely overwhelmed Joseph. He stepped down quickly from the platform, threw his arms around his youngest brother Benjamin and wept once again, this time for pure joy. Benjamin embraced his brother, lost for so

Staring in silence

long and now somehow found once again, and he too wept for joy.

Joseph kissed all his brothers, as the Hebrews did on very joyous occasions, and wept over each one of them. He was reunited with them as their brother, at long last.

"I have dreamed of this moment for years!" he exclaimed.

"Brother, that is one dream of yours we are happy to hear about," said Reuben, and they all laughed together.

Then the brothers spent several hours together talking of many things. When Pharaoh heard that Joseph's brothers had come to Egypt, he was pleased and sent word to Joseph, "Tell your brothers, 'Do this: Load your animals and return to the land of Canaan, and bring your father and your families back to me. I will give you the best of the land of Egypt and you can enjoy the fat of the land.'

"I have dreamed of this moment for years!"

"Also tell them, 'Take some carts from Egypt for your children and your wives, and get your father and come right back to the land of Egypt. Never mind about your belongings, because the best of all Egypt will be yours.'" And Joseph told his brothers all that the king of Egypt had said for them to do.

So Joseph's brothers agreed to do as Pharaoh had said. Joseph gave each of them carts and supplies for the journey, but to Benjamin he gave three hundred coins of silver and five sets of clothes. To his father, Jacob, Joseph sent ten donkeys loaded with the best products of the land of Egypt, and ten donkeys carrying the things Jacob would need for this journey down to Egypt from the land of Canaan. These donkeys carried grain, bread, and many other supplies, because it took many long days to journey on the back of a donkey from Egypt to Canaan.

Provisions for their journey

Joseph sent his brothers off saying, "Don't argue on the way!" They departed on the long trip and spent many days journeying back to their father, Jacob, in Canaan.

Journeying back to Canaan

"Joseph is still alive!"

8

ANSWERED PRAYER

When the eleven brothers returned safely to Jacob in Canaan, he was greatly relieved to see them. But he could not believe it when they said, "Joseph is still alive! In fact, he is ruler of all Egypt!" But after he had seen all the things they had brought back and the twenty donkeys sent by Joseph especially for him, his heart was gladdened.

"I'm convinced!" he exclaimed. "My son Joseph is still alive. I will go and see him before I die."

Several days were needed to prepare for the journey, since Jacob and all his sons and daughters and all their spouses and children would be leaving Canaan, never to return. But before too long, everything was ready, and they set off for Egypt with Jacob leading them.

When they reached the encampment of Beersheba, Jacob offered sacrifices to God just as his father, Isaac, had done. God spoke to Jacob (whom God had renamed Israel when Jacob wrestled with God), and said, "Jacob! Jacob!"

"Here I am," replied Jacob.

"I am God, the God of your father," He said. "Do not be afraid to go down to Egypt, for I will make you a great nation there. I will go down to Egypt with you, and I will surely bring your descendants back out of there at a later time, a great and powerful nation. And when you die, your beloved son Joseph will close your eyes with his own hand." These words were a great comfort to Jacob, because he remembered the promises God had made beforehand and knew that God would keep His promise.

The family again packed up their belongings

"Here I am."

and headed for Egypt, because Jacob was eager to see his long-lost son. The group left Beersheba, traveling in the carts that Pharaoh had given the sons when they left Egypt to get Jacob and bring him back. Jacob's family—his sons and daughters, his grandchildren, and even a few great-grandchildren, all went down to Egypt with Jacob when he decided to leave Canaan. They took all the things they owned, including all their sheep, cattle, and other livestock. Jacob took down to Egypt his sons Reuben, Simeon, Levi, Judah, Issachar, Zebulun, Gad, Asher, Dan, Naphtali, and Benjamin, his daughter Dinah, and all their children. All together, sixty-six members of Jacob's family went down to Egypt.

Jacob told his son Judah to go on ahead of the main party of travelers, so that Judah could make sure that they were going in the

Jacob's family moving to Egypt

right direction and would reach Egypt as they planned. It was difficult in those days to cross large areas of desert and wastelands and make sure that you were always headed in the right direction. So Judah went ahead just to make sure. The group had done a good job, however, and would soon arrive at the region of Goshen at the border of Egypt. When Joseph heard they would soon reach Goshen, he traveled to Goshen in his personal chariot to meet his father.

When father and son met again after so many years, Joseph ran to Jacob and gave him a big hug. For a long time he just hugged his father and wept.

After hugging his father for a very long time, Joseph stepped back, looked into Jacob's eyes, and smiled.

"Somehow, I always believed that I would see you again, Father! I had faith that our God would allow it to come to pass."

Going to meet Jacob

"I had no reason for my hope, my son, since I was told that you had been killed," said Jacob, "yet I continued to hope that somehow it wasn't true. I have prayed every day that you might somehow be restored to me. And now, after many long years, I have finally had my prayers answered. Now I am ready to die in peace, since I have seen for myself that you are still alive."

"Let us rejoice together, all of us, to be together again after all that has happened," said Levi, "and let us not fail to give thanks to our God!"

Then Joseph said to all Jacob's family that was assembled there, "I will go up and say to Pharaoh, 'My family who were living in Canaan have come to me. The men are shepherds; they tend livestock, and they have brought along their flocks and herds and everything they own.' When Pharaoh

"Let's give thanks to God."

calls you in and asks, 'What is your occupation?' you should answer, 'Your servants have tended livestock from our boyhood on, just as our fathers did.' Then you will be allowed to settle in Goshen, a rich and fertile region, because Egyptians do not like shepherds. Therefore they will be happy for all of us to settle out here at the edge of their land where they will not have to come near us too often."

And all the brothers and his father agreed on this plan.

So Joseph chose five of his brothers to present personally before Pharaoh, and took them with him to visit the king.

Pharaoh asked them, "What is your occupation?"

"Your servants are shepherds," they replied, "just as our fathers were. We have come to live here a while, because the famine

"What is your occupation?"

is severe in Canaan and your servants' flocks have no pasture. So now, please let your servants settle in Goshen."

Pharaoh then spoke to Joseph. "Your father and your brothers have come to you, and the land of Egypt is before you; settle your father and your brothers in the best part of the land. Let them live in Goshen. And if you know of any among them with special ability, put them in charge of my own livestock."

Then Pharaoh told Joseph to bring Jacob before him. The old man greeted Pharaoh according to custom, and then Pharaoh asked him, "How old are you?"

Jacob spoke slowly. "The years of my life are a hundred thirty. My years have been few and difficult, and they do not equal the years of the lives of my fathers." Pharaoh sat silently before the stooped old man who had seen so many things in his life, and who had personally

"Let them live in Goshen."

wrestled with God Almighty on a lonely riverbank many years before, and he could think of nothing else to say. So Jacob said farewell to Pharaoh and left his presence.

Joseph settled his father, his brothers and their wives and children, and his sister and her family in the region of Goshen as Pharaoh had said.

But even though Joseph was able to provide for his family that had come down from Canaan, the rest of the people of Egypt and Canaan were having a very hard time because of the famine. Over several years, they finally spent all the money they had to buy food, and still the famine continued. So the people came to Joseph and said, "Give us food so we won't die; our money is all gone."

Joseph replied, "Then bring me your livestock in exchange for more grain."

The famine continues.

The Egyptians did that until their live-stock all belonged to Pharaoh. Then they came to Joseph and said, "The famine is still going on. All we have left is our land and ourselves; make us Pharaoh's slaves so we can have more food."

So Joseph bought all the land in Egypt for his master, Pharaoh.

The people of Egypt had no choice but to become Pharaoh's slaves, since they had nothing left to sell except their land and their services. They could not hold out against the famine any longer. So all the people of Egypt became Pharaoh's slaves except for the Egyptian priests, who did not serve the Lord but served the gods of the Egyptians. Because these priests received food from Pharaoh already, they had enough to live on and did not have to sell their land or themselves to Pharaoh.

Trading livestock for food

The people of Egypt had pleaded with Joseph saying, "Give us seed so that we may live and not die, and that the land may not become desolate." Joseph had shown mercy to them and had also been faithful in doing business for his master Pharaoh by accepting their land and their services.

Joseph told the Egyptian people, "Now that I have bought you and your land today for Pharaoh, here is seed for you so you can plant the ground but when the crop comes in, give a fifth of it to Pharaoh. The other four-fifths of it you may keep as seed for the fields and as food for yourselves and your households and your children."

"You have saved our lives," the Egyptians replied. "May we find favor in the eyes of our lord; we will be in bondage to Pharaoh."

From that time onward, it became a law in the land of Egypt that the king would

"Give us seed."

receive a fifth of all the crops produced by all the people. Also, all the land of all the people except for the priests became the property of Pharaoh.

Working their crops

Jacob preparing to die

9

The Blessing

Jacob and his sons prospered greatly in Goshen, and they lived there seventeen more years, until Jacob reached the age of one hundred forty-seven. Then Jacob became aware that he would soon die. He called for his favorite son, Joseph, and spoke to him.

"If I have found favor in your eyes, put your hand under my thigh and promise that you will show me kindness and faithfulness." The people of those times would put their hand under their father's or their master's leg much like we raise our right hands today—it showed that they meant to keep their promise and were not lying.

"Do not bury me in Egypt," Jacob said, "but when I rest with my fathers, carry me out of Egypt and bury me where they are buried."

God had promised Jacob, as He had promised Jacob's father and grandfather before him, that God would make his descendants into a mighty nation. This nation would be named "Israel," the new name for Jacob that had been given to him by God Himself.

Jacob knew that God would keep this promise. Yet he wanted to be buried in the land that God had said would someday belong to this great nation Israel. So he said to Joseph, "Swear to me that you will bury me in Canaan where my fathers are buried."

"I will do as you say," said Joseph.

"Swear to me," said his father.

Then Joseph swore to his father as Jacob had asked, and when Jacob saw that his son would be faithful to carry out the promise, he worshiped God as he leaned on the top of his staff.

Jacob worshipping God

Not too long after Joseph visited his father and swore to bury him in the Promised Land, he received word that his father was sick. When they told Jacob, "Your son Joseph has come to you," he took strength and managed to sit up on his sickbed.

Jacob told his son, "God Almighty appeared to me at Luz in the land of Canaan, and there He blessed me and said to me, 'I am going to make you fruitful and will increase your numbers. I will make you a community of peoples, and I will give this land as an everlasting possession to your descendants after you.'

"Now then, your two sons born to you in Egypt before I came to you here will be counted as mine; Ephraim and Manasseh will be mine, just as my own sons Reuben and Simeon and all the others are mine."

"Any children born to you after them

Jacob became ill.

will be counted as yours and will inherit territory under the names of Ephraim and Manasseh." Then Jacob saw Ephraim and Manasseh at the far end of the room and asked Joseph, "Who are these two?"

Joseph answered, "They are the sons God has given me here in Egypt. These are Ephraim and Manasseh."

"Bring them to me so I may bless them." Blessings in those days were very important to those who received them. A blessing spoken by a man of God like Jacob was really a prophecy, a statement of what God was going to bring about in their lives.

Jacob's eyes were failing because of his great age, so that he could hardly see. So Joseph brought his sons right up to Jacob.

Jacob began by saying to Joseph, "I never expected to see your face again, and now God has allowed me to see your children, too."

Joseph's sons

Joseph then placed Manasseh, the older son, so that Jacob could put his right hand on Manasseh's head; this was the place of greater honor and belonged to the older son. But Jacob crossed his hands so that his right hand was on Ephraim's head, and his left hand on Manasseh's.

Jacob then blessed Joseph, saying, "May the God before whom my fathers walked, the God who has been Shepherd all my life to this day, the Angel who has delivered me from all harm—may He bless these boys. May they be called by my name and by the names of my fathers Abraham and Isaac, and may they increase greatly upon the earth."

At that point, Joseph noticed that his father had crossed his hands. He took his father's hands to uncross them and said, "No, my father, this one is the firstborn; put your right hand on his head."

Jacob blessing Joseph's sons

But Jacob said, "I know, my son. I know. He, too, will become a people when his descendants increase, and his name will become famous. But his younger brother will be even greater than he; his descendants will become a group of nations."

Then Jacob blessed them. "In your name will Israel pronounce this blessing: 'May God make you like Ephraim and Manasseh.'"

Then Jacob said to Joseph, "I am about to die, but God will be with you and take you back to the land of your fathers. And since you are over your brothers, I give you one portion more of the land than I am giving to your brothers.

Jacob then said, "Gather my sons around me so that I can tell them what will happen to them in the days and years to come." Jacob was a mighty man of God who could

"No, my father!"

speak the words God gave him to say, so his sons would know what would happen to them in the future. Jacob told them how the people would live who would grow up from their sons and grandsons. Their later descendants would be a mighty nation that would have the name *Israel*, inherit the Promised Land of Canaan, and make it their own.

Many of the things Jacob said were not clear to his sons, because prophets often use words in a way that could mean more than one thing. At other times they talk about animals or strange things just to show their listeners a different way of seeing things.

"Assemble and listen, sons of Jacob," he began. "Listen to your father, Israel." He then spoke to each of his sons in turn, telling them about what they had done to deserve the things that would happen to their descendants. Most of the things he described would

Sons gathering around Jacob

not take place while his sons were still alive but only after they had died.

Since Reuben, the oldest son, had done many evil things to his father over the years, he lost his rights as firstborn son. Jacob said to him, "Reuben, you are my firstborn, my might, the first sign of my strength, excelling in honor, excelling in power. Turbulent as the waters, you will no longer excel, for you sinned against me when you were younger and you will not be forgiven for it."

Jacob then called the next two in order of their birth, Simeon and Levi. Many years before, these two had taken revenge on some men who had done something wrong to their sister Dinah. But since the Lord is the one who should take revenge, Jacob had this to say to Simeon and Levi:

"Simeon and Levi are brothers—their swords are weapons of violence. Let me not

Reuben, the oldest son

enter their council, let me not join their assembly, for they have killed men in their anger and hamstrung oxen as they pleased. Cursed be their anger, so fierce, and their fury, so cruel! I will scatter them in the land of Jacob and disperse them in Israel."

Jacob spoke to them for the Lord, telling them what would happen to the tribes that would bear their names that would come in later generations.

Next, Jacob called his son Judah in front of him. Judah had often been a leader of the brothers. Jacob had many good things to say to him:

"Judah, your brothers will praise you; your hand will be on the neck of your enemies; your father's sons will bow down to you. You are a lion's cub, O Judah; you return from the prey, my son. The scepter will not depart from Judah, nor the ruler's staff from between his

"Simeon and Levi, you took revenge."

feet, until the one comes to whom it belongs and all the nations give him their obedience. He will tether his donkey to a vine, his colt to the choicest branch; he will wash his garments in wine, his robes in the blood of grapes. His eyes will be darker than wine, his teeth whiter than milk."

Jacob then spoke to Zebulun, Issachar, and Dan.

"Zebulun will live by the seashore and become a haven for ships; his border will extend toward Sidon.

"Issachar is a rawboned donkey lying down between two saddlebags. When he sees how good his resting place is, and how pleasant his land, he will bend his shoulder to the burden and submit to forced labor.

"Dan will provide justice for his people as one of the tribes of Israel. Dan will be a serpent by the roadside, a viper along the path,

Judah, father of the tribe from
which Jesus would come

that bites the horse's heels so that its rider tumbles backward. I look for your deliverance, O Lord," Jacob ended.

"Now come forth, Gad, Asher, and Naphtali, and hear the blessings I speak to you from the Lord."

"Gad will be attacked by a band of raiders, but he will attack them at their heels.

"Asher's food will be rich; he will provide delicacies fit for a king.

"Naphtali is a doe set free that bears beautiful fawns."

It was difficult for the brothers to understand just what the Lord was saying to them through these words, but most of the things Jacob had said were pleasant and seemed to mean that their tribes would do well in the Promised Land. These three brothers were pleased at what their father had told them.

"Now let Joseph, my beloved son, come forth."

Jacob continuing his blessing

Joseph stepped forward to receive his blessing, bringing Ephraim and Manasseh before Jacob, since he had said they would be treated as Jacob's own sons. "Speak your blessing to these my sons," said Joseph, "so that they may hear it."

Jacob then spoke to Joseph and his sons.

"Joseph is a fruitful vine, a fruitful vine near a spring, whose branches climb over a wall. With bitterness archers attacked him; they shot at him with hostility. But his bow remained steady, his strong arms stayed limber, because of the hand of the Mighty One of Jacob, because of the Shepherd, the Rock of Israel, because of your father's God, who helps you, because of the Almighty, who blesses you with blessings of the heavens above, blessings of the deep that lies below, blessings of the breast and womb. Your father's blessings are greater than the

Joseph and his sons

blessings of the ancient mountains, than the bounty of the age-old hills. Let all these rest on the head of Joseph, on the brow of the prince among his brothers."

Joseph was deeply moved at hearing the rich blessings God would provide to his children, especially after the years he had suffered in Egypt as a prisoner and a slave. "Thank you, Father," was all he could say.

"It is a good blessing!" all his brothers cried, "Praise the Lord for his faithfulness to Joseph!" They were glad that Joseph had received great blessings from God.

"Well, Father," said Benjamin, "as the youngest I always seem to be going last. I hope you have saved a blessing for me."

"Yes, of course, my son. Listen: Benjamin is a ravenous wolf; in the morning he devours the prey, in the evening divides the plunder."

Joseph's blessing

His brothers laughed and cheered at this prophecy; they could not picture their little brother as a ravenous wolf, no matter how hard they tried.

Cheering Benjamin

Jacob prophesying of Moses

10

JACOB'S DEATH

And so Jacob told his sons what would come to pass to the tribes of people that would grow up from all their descendants. One day several hundred years later they would be called by God to go up out of Egypt and take over the land that God had promised to Jacob's forefathers and to Jacob and his descendants. It would not happen during Jacob's lifetime, nor Joseph's, nor the lifetimes of Joseph's children or grandchildren. But in God's timing, according to God's plan, He would one day raise up a leader who would take the twelve tribes, descended from these twelve sons of Israel, and lead them into the Promised Land of Canaan. And then all these prophecies that Jacob had spoken would come to pass, because Jacob had spoken for the Lord.

Then Jacob spoke again to his sons. "I am about to be gathered to my people." By this Jacob meant he was about to die. "Bury me with my fathers in the cave in the field of Machpelah, near Mamre in Canaan, which my grandfather Abraham bought from the Hittites. That is the place where my grandfather, Abraham, and my grandmother, Sarah, are buried, and where my father, Isaac, and my mother, Rebekah, are buried, and that is where I buried my wife Leah. So please make sure you do as my son Joseph has promised me and carry my body back to Canaan to be buried with all the rest of my people."

As soon as he had finished saying these things to his sons, Jacob lay back down on the bed, took a deep breath, and died.

When Jacob's sons saw that he was dead, they tore their clothes as the Hebrews do

Jacob died.

when they are very sad, and they began to weep for their dead father. All Jacob's twelve sons, his daughter Dinah, and all their wives and children and grandchildren began to weep and mourn for the great man who had just died. Jacob was a beloved father and grandfather and the leader of their clan. Joseph flung himself down upon his father's body and began to weep in sorrow.

After some time, Joseph called for the doctors of Egypt who served him to come and prepare Jacob to be buried. These doctors spent forty days applying special lotions and herbs to the body, preparing it for burial. The Egyptians mourned seventy days for Jacob according to their customs.

Once the time of mourning had passed, Joseph spoke to those in Pharaoh's court. "If I have found favor in your eyes," he said, "speak to Pharaoh for me. Tell him that my father made

Joseph weeping for his father

me swear an oath and said, 'I am about to die; bury me in the tomb I dug for myself in the land of Canaan.' Ask him to let me go up and bury my father; then I will return."

After several days of waiting, some of the people in Pharaoh's court found the right time to speak to him about Joseph's request. They told him what Joseph had asked, then said, "O great king, please grant the request of your good servant Joseph, for you know how he loved his father."

And Pharaoh sent this message to Joseph: "Go up and bury your father, as he made you swear to do."

Joseph then made preparations to return to Canaan to bury his father. Pharaoh sent a huge delegation of his most important officials, all those from his own personal court and all the other officials of Egypt.

Besides all of the Egyptians, of course,

Granting Joseph's request

all of Jacob's family went back with Joseph to Canaan. All the members of Joseph's household, all his brothers, and all of Jacob's own household went back to Canaan for Jacob's burial. They left only the youngest children in Egypt—everybody else made the trip back for the burial. Also, many chariots and riders on horseback made the trip, because Jacob was a very important man, and Pharaoh wanted to honor him with a large group of people at his funeral. They all gathered together and left for Canaan.

After many days of hot travel on the dusty roads on horses, on donkeys, and in chariots and wagons, the travelers reached Atad, a village near the Jordan River. When they reached the place where farmers threshed their wheat at Atad, Joseph and the others began to weep again for Jacob. So the group stopped there for seven days to hold a ceremony of mourning for Jacob. This village

Funeral procession

was in the land of Canaan, so the people there thought all these people coming up from Egypt were Egyptians—they didn't know that many of them had once lived in Canaan. So the local people renamed the place "Abel Mizraim," which in the Hebrew language means "mourning of the Egyptians." After seven days, the group left for Mamre.

They buried Jacob in the land of Canaan, as he had made Joseph swear to do. They brought him from Egypt into the land of Canaan and went to the village of Mamre. Near that village was the cave of Machpelah, which Jacob's grandfather, Abraham, had bought from the Hittite man named Ephron. Abraham bought the field near the cave, as well as the cave for a burial place, and Jacob's grandmother, grandfather, and both his parents were buried there. Canaan was the land that God had promised to Abraham, then to

Burying Jacob

his son Isaac, and then again to Jacob. Jacob wanted to be buried in this Promised Land with his forefathers.

After they had buried Jacob in Canaan near Mamre, Joseph and his brothers and all the others went back to Egypt.

Once Joseph's brothers saw that Jacob was no longer around to protect them from Joseph, they became afraid. They thought it had only been because of their father that Joseph had not taken revenge on them before. So they made up a message, pretending that Jacob had said it before he died. They hoped that Joseph would honor his father's words. But Jacob never actually said it—the brothers just made it up. The message was, "This is what your father Jacob said: 'I ask you to forgive your brothers the sins and the wrongs they committed in treating you so badly.'

Secret meeting

Now please forgive the sins of the servants of the God of your father."

When Joseph heard what the brothers were trying to do, he was very sad that they were still afraid. He wanted them to know that they were forgiven already. Joseph wept.

Joseph's brothers then came to him and again bowed low to the ground before him, saying, "We are your slaves."

But Joseph replied, "Don't be afraid of me any longer. Am I in the place of God that I should take revenge on you for what you did? I know that you meant to do me evil, but God meant it for good, to accomplish what is now being done. Because I was here at the right time to make God's will known in the matter of the dream and the famine, many lives here in Egypt have been saved. So then, don't be afraid. I will provide for all of you and all your children."

Telling a false message

Joseph made it very clear to his brothers that he had forgiven them for everything they had done. He spoke very kindly to all of them.

"You meant to do me evil."

Goshen meadows

11

A Great Nation

Joseph spent the rest of his life in Egypt, as a very important man and a servant and official under the king. He served in Pharaoh's court for many years and was greatly loved by all those in Pharaoh's household. He and his brothers saw each other and their families often and lived happily in Egypt. Pharaoh had given them the land of Goshen, one of the richest parts of Egypt. Goshen had green fields, rolling meadows full of grass for their cattle and sheep, and plenty of water. All Jacob's family did very well and were quite happy in their new home.

Joseph himself lived to be a hundred and ten years old. He lived so long that he got to see the birth of his great-great grandchildren, something very few people live to see.

Then one day, Joseph said to his brothers, many of whom had also lived to a great old age, "I am about to die. But God will surely come to your aid and take you up out of this land to the land He promised on oath to Abraham, Isaac, and Jacob."

Joseph then made his brothers, the sons of Israel, swear an oath to him. He told them, "God will surely come to your aid and bring you out of Egypt. And when He does, you must carry my bones up from this place." His brothers understood that Joseph was speaking about a much later time, and that he did not mean that they would be carrying his bones. Joseph knew that any promise his brothers made would be carried out by their descendants. So he asked his brothers, and they swore it to him.

In asking this of his brothers, Joseph was showing great faith in God. It takes a lot of

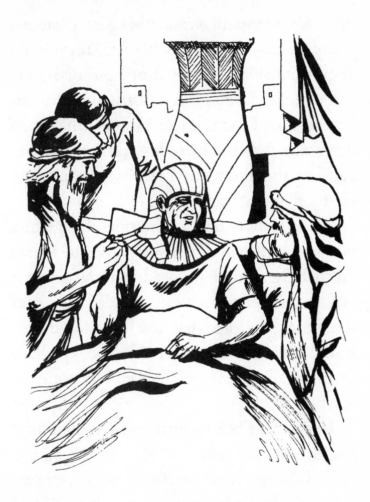

"Do not leave my bones in Egypt."

faith to believe that something will happen many years after you will die! Yet Joseph knew that whatever the Lord promises, He will do! So Joseph gave instructions to his brothers, and made them promise that their descendants would carry his bones with them back to the Promised Land whenever God led them back from Egypt.

Then Joseph died, at the ripe old age of a hundred and ten. The Egyptians and all his brothers held a long period of mourning for him, just as they had for his father Jacob. And the Egyptians prepared his body for burial, a skill they had that Hebrews did not have then. Finally Joseph was buried in a coffin in Egypt.

Joseph had been a great man, a man used mightily by the Lord. Why was Joseph, the son of Jacob, used by God to do mighty things for Him, like interpreting dreams and

Preparing Joseph's body for burial

leading all of Egypt through a seven-year famine? Mostly it was because Joseph had great faith in God. He believed that God was able and willing to help him and to protect him wherever he went, whether it was in a deep dark cistern or a prison cell in a foreign country. He trusted God to take care of him even when it looked like things weren't going too well.

Joseph also knew it was very important to always do the right thing, even if it was not always the easy thing or the thing other people wanted him to do. Joseph knew that God expects us to try to be faithful to Him, just as He is always faithful to us.

And, as it turned out, Joseph was right when he said that God would bring Israel back out of Egypt and into the Promised Land. About four hundred years after Joseph died, an evil pharaoh rose up who did not

Joseph had been faithful to God.

remember Joseph and all the things he had done for Egypt. This pharaoh hated the people called Israelites and made them slaves. But God raised up another man, just as he raised up Joseph to take care of His people. This man, named Moses, did many miracles and led God's chosen people out from the land where they had become slaves. After many adventures and wandering around in the wilderness for forty years, the people of Israel came once again to the Promised Land, which they had left in Joseph's time, more than four hundred years before.

But before they left Egypt, Moses made sure the people of Israel got Joseph's bones out of the grave where they had been lying for so many years. Moses made sure that Joseph's bones were carried wherever they went as they wandered through the wilderness, even though it would have been easier to leave them behind.

Moses

And finally, when the people of Israel entered the Promised Land, they carried Joseph's bones and laid them to rest with the graves of his family, just as he had wanted and as he had made his brothers swear so long ago. Joseph had known even then that the promise God had made to his great-grandfather, Abraham, to his grandfather Isaac, and to his father, Jacob, would be kept. And God did keep His promise and made Israel a great nation in their land.

Burying Joseph with his ancestors

GLOSSARY

Bereaved: one who has lost a loved one; very sad.

Bondage: slavery.

Caravan: a group of people traveling together.

Cistern: an open pit for catching and storing rainwater.

Deliverance: saving someone from danger.

Desolate: ruined, destroyed or wasted; empty.

Divination: talking to evil spirits or using magic to see the future.

Famine: widespread lack of food where many people go hungry or starve.

Innocence: not having done anything wrong; not guilty.

Interpret (interpreter, interpretation): to explain; one who explains; an explanation.

Mourning: a time or feeling of sadness, usually when a loved one dies.

Parched: very dry.

Prophet (prophecy, prophesied): prophets speak for God and tell the future, called prophesying or telling a prophecy.

Protest: to strongly say something.

Repent: to be sorry about something and stop doing it.

Sackcloth: a type of rough cloth not used normally for clothes but worn when mourning by the Hebrews.

Sin: to do something that God does not want us to do.

Steward: someone in charge of something (such as money or a house) for someone else.

Weep (wept): to cry (cried).

Withered: dead from having no water.